# A Little French Cookbook

## Janet Laurence

### ILLUSTRATED BY DIANA LEADBETTER

First published by
The Appletree Press Ltd, 7 James Street South,
Belfast BT2 8DL. Text © Janet Laurence, 1989.
Illustrations © Diana Leadbetter, 1989.
Printed in the E.C. All rights reserved.
No part of this publication may be
reproduced or transmitted in any form or
by any means, electronic or mechanical,
photocopying, recording or any information
and retrieval system, without permission in
writing from the publisher

First published in the United States in 1989
by Chronicle Books, 275 Fifth Street,
San Francisco, CA 94103

ISBN: 0-87701-642-9

9 8 7 6 5 4

# Introduction

French cuisine is rightly regarded as one of the richest in the world and this little book cannot do much more than present a few of the best known traditional dishes. Yet I think they add up to a repertoire that most would be happy to eat day after day. Once easily available in any number of modest restaurants, today they are more often found in the home; all the more reason, then, to cook them yourself!

## A note on measures

Imperial, metric and volume measurements have been used for all the recipes. Follow one set only as they are not necessarily exact equivalents. Where no volume measurement is given, as for meat weights, for instance, use the metric rather than the imperial measurement. The cup is the standard American one of 8 fl oz. Tablespoons are the current standard measurements with the spoon levelled off. Recipes are for four unless otherwise stated. Finally, most of these recipes depend on choice of top quality ingredients and careful flavouring for good results. Do taste as you go along and adjust seasoning, etc., as you prefer.

# Croissants · Café au Lait

No French breakfast is complete without flaky croissants and milky coffee drunk from an enormous cup, sometimes without a handle. By baking your own, you can ensure that they are made with butter.

| | |
|---|---|
| 4 cups bread flour | 4 tbsp grapeseed or |
| 2 tsp salt | peanut oil |
| 1 package (1 tbsp) active | 1 cup unsalted butter |
| dry yeast | straight from |
| 1 cup warm milk | refrigerator |
| | 1 beaten egg |

Stir yeast into flour sifted with salt. Mix together milk and oil, add to flour then knead very lightly until dough is reasonably smooth, but stopping before elasticity develops. Place in covered bowl and leave until doubled in size. Divide butter into four and work each quarter with a metal spatula knife until pliable. Punch down dough, knead briefly then roll out on floured surface to 10 inch x 16 inch. Dot first quarter of butter on top two thirds of pastry, leaving margin. Fold unbuttered bottom third onto middle, then the top, buttered third over this. Seal open sides with edge of hand. Wrap in plastic wrap and let rest in refrigerator 30 minutes.

Place open edge at right angles to table edge, roll out to same size rectangle and repeat until all butter added. Roll out and fold again. Cut in half then roll out each half to a

out and fold again. Cut in half then roll out each half to a square the thickness of ⅛ in or 2 mm. Cut each square into four, then each quarter into two triangles. Roll each triangle lightly, elongating its point, then roll it up loosely from the base. Place spread apart on greased baking tray with ends curved in to form a crescent with the point inside the curve and underneath croissant. Cover with oiled film or damp cloth and leave until well risen. Brush with beaten egg and bake in pre-heated oven at gas mark 8, 220°C, 425°F for 10-15 minutes until risen and golden brown. Cool on a rack for 10 mins before eating.

**Café au Lait** The best coffee is made with freshly roasted beans, ground just before use. Quantity will depend on desired strength and the finer the coffee is ground the more flavour it will yield. Approximately 1 tablespoon to a scant half pint/250 ml/1 cup of water is a good starting point for strong coffee. Place grounds in a warmed jug or cafetière, allow boiling water to cool for ten seconds then pour over grounds. Stir coffee then leave to infuse for five minutes. Strain into a clean warm jug or push down cafetière plunger. Have an equal quantity of milk just below boiling point and pour into cup at same time as the coffee.

# Mimosa

This is a deliciously simple drink that calls for good champagne and freshly squeezed orange juice. Sparkling white wine and diluted frozen juice won't produce nearly such a good drink. Outside France it is occasionally known as Buck's Fizz. Drunk in the South of France under a hot spring sun when the tiny yellow balls of the mimosa trees fill the air with their slightly spicy fragrance, it is irresistible. Elsewhere it is still one of the most refreshing of all alcoholic drinks and a superb way to start the day. Just mix equal quantities of chilled champagne and fresh orange juice and serve in chilled glasses.

# Croque Monsieur

An ideal snack. Croque Madame adds a fried egg on top.

| | |
|---|---|
| 8 slices good white bread, cut fairly thinly | 1 tbsp French mustard |
| | 4 thin slices ham |
| 8 thin slices Gruyère cheese | 1 small egg, lightly beaten |
| | 2 oz/50 g/¼ cup butter |

Spread each slice of bread with a little mustard then make sandwiches with a slice of ham placed in the middle of two slices of cheese, pressing together well. Cut in half if liked. Dip each sandwich briefly in the egg then fry in the butter until golden on both sides. Serve immediately. The Croque Monsieur are sometimes served with cheese sauce but I prefer them as they are, garnished with a little parsley. This can be fried as well if liked.

Sometimes these sandwiches are fried in butter without being dipped first in the beaten egg. Either version is excellent.

# Omelette

Lightness is all in making an omelette, achieved by using water with the eggs, beating until just amalgamated and cooking very quickly.

---

2 eggs    salt & black pepper
1 dsp cold water    small knob of butter

**Suggested Fillings**

1 large tbsp chopped fresh herbs
diced ham
2 tbsp grated cheese
a little meat or mushrooms in sauce
(serves one)

---

Beat eggs with water and seasoning until just amalgamated, about 30 strokes with a fork. Add herbs or diced ham. Heat pan, add butter and swirl round as it melts. As soon as frothing stops, add omelette mixture in one go. Start moving pan across heat and use fork to move cooked mixture away from bottom of pan, allowing liquid, uncooked mixture to run underneath. For other flavours, add grated cheese or heated sauce across middle of omelette whilst top is still runny. Flip top third of omelette over filling and leave for a few seconds for bottom to brown slightly. Have hot plate ready to hand, shake pan to loosen omelette, then slide it onto plate, tilting pan so it ends up fully rolled. A little chopped parsley provides a nice finish. Eat immediately.

# Salade Niçoise

One of those recipes that generate much debate over the correct ingredients. Tomatoes, anchovies, hard-boiled eggs, olives and basil are essential. Escoffier added tuna fish in oil. Green beans, or artichoke hearts, and green peppers are usual and after that you are on your own. A really fruity olive oil to dress the salad is also essential; the country round Nice produces some of the best. Whether the oil is used on its own or in a vinaigrette dressing can be another source of contention but in France garlic is usually included either way. Forget the arguments and just enjoy this delicious dish.

---

*1 small crisp lettuce,*    *6-8 anchovy fillets*
*shredded*    *8-10 sweet black olives*
*4 firm tomatoes, peeled, quartered, deseeded, salted*
*and drained*
*2 hard-boiled eggs, peeled and quartered*
*1 green pepper, shredded*
*handful green beans, cooked lightly in salted water*
*French dressing made with tarragon vinegar, extra virgin*
*olive oil, salt & freshly ground black pepper*
*a crushed clove of garlic*
*few basil leaves*

---

Place lettuce in bottom of bowl or shallow dish, arrange the drained tomatoes, eggs, pepper, beans, anchovies and olives on top. At the last minute sprinkle with dressing and tear the basil leaves over.

# Quiche Lorraine

The traditional quiche comes from Lorraine in the North of France and never contains onion. Sometimes a little Gruyère cheese is added with the bacon but not by purists. Heavy cream would have been used originally but half-and-half, or a mixture of cream and milk, can be used very successfully.

---

### Shortcrust Pastry

| | |
|---|---|
| scant 1½ cups flour | ½ cup butter |
| good pinch salt | 2 tbsp ice-cold water |

### Filling

| | |
|---|---|
| ½ cup unsmoked lean bacon, cut in strips | 1 cup cream |
| a little butter | salt, freshly ground black pepper & grating |
| 3 large eggs, lightly beaten | nutmeg |

---

Sift flour with salt, rub in butter to breadcrumb stage, sprinkle with ice-cold water and mix lightly to a firm dough, adding a little more water if necessary. Leave to rest for 20 minutes then roll out quite thinly and line 8-inch flan tin with removable bottom. Chill then blind bake in moderately hot oven, 375°F, for 20 minutes. Meanwhile, fry the bacon for a few minutes in a little butter until just brown (if using the more traditional smoked bacon, blanch in boiling water for a few minutes then dry before frying). Arrange on bottom of flan after removing from oven. Lightly whip eggs and cream until completely mixed, season (take into account saltiness of bacon) then fill pastry shell. Replace in oven and bake for further 25-30 minutes, until filling is puffy and a sharp knife point inserted in centre will emerge clean. Eat warm or cold.

# Crudités à l'Aïoli

Crudités are slim sticks of raw vegetable. Strips of carrot and peppers, florets of cauliflower, pieces of cucumber, anything crunchy can be used to dip in the wonderful, garlicky mayonnaise. Serve with drinks, particularly on a sunny terrace, or as a light lunch.

---

2 large cloves garlic, peeled     ½ tsp fine sea-salt
I large egg yolk    a little water
freshly ground white or black pepper
½ cup virgin olive oil

---

Crush garlic cloves by scraping them down into the salt with a small, sharp knife, working away until a creamy paste is produced. Put this into a smallish bowl, add egg yolk and beat until pale light, then add pepper. Add oil drop by drop, beating all the time (by electric beater if you like). If mixture becomes too thick to work, add a teaspoon of hot water. After half oil has been incorporated, it can be added a little more rapidly.

# Poireaux à la Grecque

Despite the name, this is a favourite French method of cooking vegetables. Mushrooms, eggplant, zucchini, small onions, etc, can be done the same way. The length of cooking for each will vary. Serve as a starter, with other items for a composed salad, or use a selection for an attractive hors d'oeuvre.

---

*5 cups water*
*1 cup olive oil*
*3 tbsp fresh lemon juice*
*3 tbsp chopped shallots or green onions*
*12 parsley stalks, 1 celery stalk, 1 sprig fennel (or 1/4 tsp fennel seeds), 1 sprig thyme (or 1/4 tsp dried thyme), 20 peppercorns, 15 coriander seeds, 2 crushed cloves garlic, 1/2 tsp salt*
*1 1/2 lbs young leeks, trimmed, washed and tied*

---

Place all ingredients except leeks in a saucepan and bring gently to the boil. Add cleaned and tied leeks and bring back to boil then cover and simmer gently until leeks tender (if preferred, this can be done in a preheated oven, 350°F, approximately 1 hour). When leeks are done, remove and reduce liquid to about 1 cup then strain over leeks and chill before serving.

# Pâté de Campagne

Every French housewife has her own favourite recipe for this coarse-textured pâté. This is one of my favourites.

---

*1½ lbs boned side pork minced*
*4 oz pork fat, diced*
*6 oz breast of chicken, diced*
*12 oz pig's liver, minced*
*1 large onion, finely chopped, cooked to transparency in*
*2 tbsp butter*
*2 eggs, beaten*
*4 tbsp fine white breadcrumbs*
*2 cloves garlic, crushed*
*10 black peppercorns, ½ tsp green peppercorns,*
*5 juniper berries, all crushed, good pinch mixed*
*charcuterie spices, good grating nutmeg,*
*1½ tsp salt, 3 tbsp chopped parsley, 2 bay leaves*
*½ cup dry white wine*
*8 oz unsmoked bacon cut thinly*
*(serves 6-8)*

---

Combine all ingredients except bacon and bay leaves, mix well and leave for flavours to mature for several hours, or overnight if convenient. Place one bay leaf in the bottom of a 2½-3 pint terrine then line with the bacon, stretched with the back of a knife, leaving ends hanging over the edge of the dish. Fill with the pâté mixture, piling it up in the centre and placing the other bay leaf on top. Flip over the

ends of the bacon and use any over to cover top. Place in a dish containing 1 inch hot water and cook in a preheated oven at 325°F, for approximately 2 hours. Pâté is cooked when it has shrunk from side of dish, an inserted skewer emerges hot and clean and pâté feels firm to touch. Cool for an hour on a rack then weight lightly overnight.

# Salade Verte

The traditional vinaigrette is one part vinegar to three parts oil with only salt and pepper for seasoning. For many people that is slightly too acid and the following version uses more oil and a touch of French mustard and sugar. The only essentials are to have first class wine vinegar and oil. Only sufficient dressing to gloss each salad item should be used; apply and toss immediately before eating.

| | |
|---|---|
| *½ tsp French mustard* | *10 tbsp oil, olive or any* |
| *1 tsp superfine sugar* | *good unrefined variety* |
| *salt & freshly ground black* | *crushed clove garlic,* |
| *pepper* | *chopped herbs* |
| *2 tbsp wine vinegar* | *(optional)* |

Mix the mustard with the sugar, add seasoning and vinegar, mixing well. Add the oil, whisking in, and use immediately or whisk again before using. It will keep in a screw-topped jar in the refrigerator, ready to be shaken for use.

# Soufflé au Fromage

The soufflé is the quintessence of French cooking, depending on careful technique and subtle flavouring to produce a dish that wins plaudits every time. And in truth it is not as difficult to make as it appears!

| | |
|---|---|
| 4 tbsp butter | 1 tsp Dijon mustard |
| ½ cup flour | salt, freshly ground black |
| 1 cup milk | pepper, good pinch |
| 6 tbsp dry white wine | cayenne pepper |
| 1 cup grated Gruyère cheese | 5 large egg whites |
| 4 large egg yolks | |

Butter well a large soufflé dish (9 cup capacity) and dust with a little cayenne pepper. Melt butter, add flour then liquids to make a smooth sauce. Remove from heat, add cheese then beat in egg yolks one by one. Add mustard and seasonings to taste. Finally beat egg whites to stiff peak, fold in one-third then add mixture to remaining egg whites, carefully folding in. Three-quarters fill soufflé dish, levelling off top. Place in preheated oven at 375°F for 30 minutes, then give dish a careful shake. If the soufflé wobbles, give it another few minutes; if it just trembles, serve immediately. Plunge two spoons back to back into the centre then ensure each serving has a combination of soft centre and crisp outside.

# Moules Marinière

Moules, or mussels, are found all along the Normandy and Breton coasts and nearly every restaurant offers a version of this famous dish.

| | |
|---|---|
| 4 lbs live mussels, scrubbed | ½ cup dry white wine plus same amount water |
| I large onion, chopped | |
| 4-5 sprigs parsley, small sprig thyme | 2 tbsp butter, cut in small dice |
| freshly ground pepper | 2 tbsp lemon juice |
| 4 tbsp butter | 2 tbsp chopped parsley |

Clean and scrape mussels thoroughly, discarding any that won't close. Place onion, sprigs of parsley and thyme and black pepper in wide, thick-bottomed pan. Add the first lot of butter, the wine and the water. Place half mussels on top, cover and place over a high heat for a few minutes, shaking the pan every now and then so mussels cook evenly. Check after two minutes and remove mussels as they open. Discard half of each shell, placing remaining shell and mussel in warm serving dish. Keep warm. Discard any mussels that don't open. Repeat with remaining mussels. When all mussels removed, strain juices very well and reduce to a half. Whisk in the diced butter off the heat so the liquid thickens slightly then whisk in lemon juice. Check seasoning, adding a little salt if necessary; add chopped parsley. Pour over mussels and serve immediately.

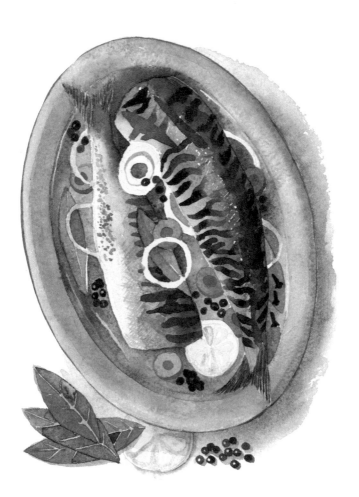

# Filets de Maquereau

In the North of France, where the Atlantic yields fine mackerel, this dish is very popular and usually served as one of a selection of hors d'oeuvres.

---

*1 cup dry white wine*
*1 cup water*
*1 medium-sized onion, sliced; 1 carrot, sliced;*
*6 peppercorns; 4 coriander seeds; few sprigs parsley or*
*fennel, tied with a bay leaf; little salt*
*4 mackerel, gutted and cleaned*
*juice 1 lemon*
*parsley or fennel for garnishing*

---

Place wine, water and seasonings in a saucepan, bring to the boil and simmer for 10 minutes. Place the cleaned mackerel in a flameproof dish, squeeze over the lemon juice then pour over the hot liquid plus all the flavourings. Add vegetables. Cover with tin foil, bring to simmering point then lower heat slightly and poach very gently for about 10 minutes until fish is just cooked. Remove from heat, transfer to serving dish, pour over liquid and flavourings, discarding soggy herbs, and allow to cool. Garnish with fresh herbs before serving. If preferred, fish can be skinned and filleted when cold and served with about half of the liquid mixed with a little French mustard.

# Bouillabaisse

There are those who say Bouillabaisse cannot be cooked outside the Mediterranean area as the right fish are not available. Substitutions do not give the authentic flavour but still produce an excellent dish. Good olive oil, though, really is essential.

---

4½ lbs mixed fish containing sculpin (red scorpionfish), red mullet or searobin; monkfish, conger or moray eel; whiting or flatfish; wrasse; some small crustacea such as shrimp or mantis prawns (exact proportions not vital but important to have some fish from each group); all fish to be gutted, scaled and in large-ish chunks

| | |
|---|---|
| 1 cup good olive oil | 10 cups boiling water |
| 1 large onion, finely sliced | few strands saffron, 3 |
| 2 cloves garlic, crushed | tbsp freshly chopped |
| 1 lb tasty tomatoes, or 1 | parsley |
| tbsp tomato purée | salt & black pepper |

**Rouille**

2 cloves garlic, 2 sweet red peppers, finely chopped
1 small white loaf, decrusted, soaked in milk and squeezed dry
2 tbsp olive oil   1 cup fish stock
(serves 6)

---

Heat half olive oil in large saucepan, add onion and garlic and cook gently until transparent. Add tomatoes, seasoning, boiling water and all fish except whiting or

flatfish and very small crustacea. Bring back to boil, pour over remaining olive oil and cook at a vigorous bubble for some 15 minutes. Then add the reserved fish and continue boiling until they are just cooked, adding the saffron and parsley just before the end.

To serve, for each person have garlic-rubbed pieces of toast in one bowl, place the pieces of fish which are still whole in another, then pour the broth over the toast. Hand round the rouille separately.

**Rouille** Pound garlic and red peppers in a mortar or process. Add bread and work together. Then add olive oil and sufficient stock to make a sauce the consistency of mayonnaise. A little anchovy essence can be added for extra pungency.

# Pot au Feu

A dish that is in the repertoire of every French provincial housewife. This recipe uses beef top round but it is very adaptable. Leftovers are delicious cold.

---

*9 pts beef stock & water, or water*
*4 tsp sea-salt, 24 black peppercorns*
*4½ lbs beef top round, fat free, tied neatly*
*2-3 pieces shin bone, preferably with some meat,*
*blanched for 5 minutes*
*3 leeks, 3 carrots, 4 celery stalks, 2 onions, all large, all*
*cleaned and cut in half*

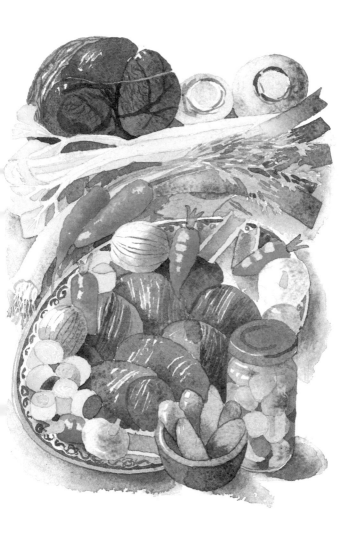

*I bay leaf, 4 sprigs parsley with stalk, I sprig thyme, all
tied together (bouquet garni)
selection vegetables: small leeks, small onions, carrots,
young turnips, celery, potatoes, etc, all cleaned, cut into
serving pieces and trimmed if necessary
parsley for garnish
(serves 8-10)*

---

Bring stock, stock and water, or water to boil in large pot. Add prepared meat and bones and bring back to boil, skimming off scum as it rises. Add first lot of vegetables, herbs and seasonings. Cover, leaving lid slightly ajar so steam can escape, reducing heat so liquid no more than trembles. Cook until meat is tender, approximately 3½-4 hours. If adding more than one piece of meat to the pot, allow time for heat to return to poaching point. Long thin pieces of meat will cook more quickly than more solid shapes. Meat is ready when a knife slips in easily. Discard vegetables cooked with meat and either cook second lot in stock, timing their addition so all are ready at the same time as the meat, or separately.

Keep cooked meat and vegetables warm. Degrease stock then strain. Reduce if necessary; check seasoning. Slice meat and arrange on a dish, surrounding with second lot of vegetables; pour a little stock over. Serve some of remaining stock in soup bowls. Then serve the meat and vegetables garnished with a little parsley and accompanied by coarse sea salt, pickled onions and some gherkins.

# Boeuf à la Bourguignonne

Burgundy is one of the great wine regions of France producing a variety of wines ranging from light and fresh to great and complex. This famous casserole is now cooked all over the country and though a good robust Burgundy produces a memorable result, a less expensive red wine will serve as long as it is drinkable.

---

*1 large onion, sliced   12-18 button mushrooms*
*2 tbsp olive oil   1 tbsp butter*
*bouquet garni   2 tbsp brandy*
*2 lbs stewing steak, cut into 2-inch pieces*
*2½ cups red Burgundy*
*2 tbsp beef dripping or lard or oil*
*4 oz piece unsmoked bacon, cut into small strips*
*12 small, pickling onions, peeled*
*2 tbsp flour, well seasoned with salt & black pepper*
*approx. 1 cup beef stock*
*2 cloves garlic, lightly crushed*
*2 tbsp chopped fresh parsley*

---

Place meat in a bowl or plastic bag, add onion, oil and wine, push in bouquet garni, and leave for 3-6 hours. Heat fat in flameproof casserole then add strips of bacon and the pickling onions, cooking gently. Remove bacon when fat is transparent and the onions when golden. Remove meat from marinade, dry carefully on kitchen paper then brown on all sides. Sprinkle flour over all meat in

casserole, stirring to absorb fat. Cover meat with strained marinade and stock. Add bouquet garni and garlic. Bring to boil then cover and place in preheated oven at 325°F for 2 hours.

Heat butter and cook mushrooms until moisture evaporates and add to casserole along with browned bacon and onions. Cook for a further 30 minutes or until meat is tender. Let casserole stand for few minutes, skim off fat and remove bouquet garni and garlic. Flame brandy, stir into casserole and cook gently on top of stove for a couple of minutes then place in serving dish, garnish with chopped parsley and serve. Steamed potatoes are a traditional accompaniment but rice or creamed potatoes are equally suitable.

# Cassoulet

Like many regional dishes, fierce argument wages over the exact ingredients of Cassoulet. Confit d'oie, preserved goose, is considered essential by some; others hold that beans, pork and sausages were the only original ingredients.

*1¾ lbs dried large white beans*
*10 oz salt pork*
*4 lightly-crushed cloves garlic*
*2½ lbs boned pork spare rib*
*2½ lbs boned shoulder of lamb*

*salt & freshly ground pepper*
*I cup white breadcrumbs*
*I large onion, peeled, 2 carrots, scrubbed, bouquet of herbs, tied*
*I lb Toulouse or French garlic sausage, preferably for boiling*
*(serves 8-10)*

---

Remove rind from both pieces of pork and cut into small squares. Rinse beans well, cover with water, bring to boil, remove from heat, leave for I hour then drain and rinse well. Re-cover generously with water, add squares of rind, salt pork, onion, carrots, bouquet garni and garlic; bring to boil then simmer about I ½ hours or until beans are just tender. Meanwhile season and roast the lamb and retied spare rib in a preheated oven, 350°F, until just cooked, about I ½ hours. If using Toulouse sausage, roast with the meat for 20 minutes. A boiling sausage should be added to the beans.

Drain and reserve liquid from cooked beans, discard onion, herbs and garlic. Place half beans and rind in bottom of large casserole, add all meats, cut into serving pieces, cover with remaining beans and season if required. Pour over 2 cups of reserved liquid and add a layer of breadcrumbs. Place in preheated oven at 275°F for I ½ hours. After half an hour stir in breadcrumbs, adding more liquid if mixture seems at all dry. Add more breadcrumbs. Repeat process again after 30 minutes. At the end of cooking, beans should be moist and creamy, meats meltingly tender and crumb crust golden and crisp. Serve with a green salad.

# Faisan Normand

Normandy is famous for butter, cream, apples, cider and the apple brandy known as Calvados. These ingredients are used in a number of dishes, all called after the district. This is a very good way of cooking pheasant, which can sometimes be rather dry.

| | |
|---|---|
| 2 pheasants, trussed | 1 cup heavy cream |
| 2 tbsp butter, 1 tbsp oil | 4 eating apples, peeled |
| 4 eating apples, sliced | and diced |
| 6 tbsp Calvados or | 4 tbsp butter |
| brandy | another tbsp Calvados (or |
| juice ½ lemon, salt & | brandy) |
| pepper | chopped parsley |

Heat the butter and oil in a frying pan or skillet and brown the pheasants all over. Lay the sliced apples in a casserole dish; add the browned pheasants. Add Calvados or brandy to juices in pan and then pour over the birds. Add the lemon juice and seasoning. Cover tightly and place in a preheated oven at 350°F for 1 hour or until cooked. Towards the end of cooking time, fry the diced apples in the butter until they are golden, then keep warm.

When cooked, cut birds into pieces and place in serving dish; keep warm. Strain juices into a pan, add the cream and, stirring gently, bring to boil; add remaining tbsp of Calvados; check seasoning. Pour over the pheasants and serve with the apples in a separate dish. Garnish meat with

chopped parsley. Serve with a green vegetable or salad and new or creamed potatoes.

# Gigot qui Pleure

The 'tears' of this crying lamb are the juices which drop from the pierced leg onto the potatoes cooking beneath, producing two delicious dishes at the same time.

| | |
|---|---|
| 3½ lbs leg of lamb | ½ tsp each chopped fresh |
| 2 tbsp olive oil | rosemary and thyme |
| 2 cloves garlic, peeled and | 3½ lbs potatoes, |
| cut in slivers | peeled and sliced |
| salt & black pepper | 1 large onion, finely |
| 1 cup light stock | chopped |

Rub lamb with oil. Using a small, sharp knife, make deep incisions all over and insert a sliver of garlic in each. Season and sprinkle with the herbs. Mix potatoes with onion, season and place in lightly oiled pan. Bring stock to boil and pour over. Place leg straight onto shelf in preheated oven at 425°F and arrange the pan of potatoes underneath. Roast 1¼-1½ hours (lamb should be underdone). Stir potatoes once or twice as they cook and reduce heat if they seem to be over-browning. Allow to sit in a warm place for 20 minutes before carving. Serve with a home-made jelly and plain green vegetable or salad.

# Carré d'Agneau aux Haricots

White beans and lamb are a favourite combination.

---

2 cups dried large white
beans
2 medium sized onions
salt & black pepper
best end of rack of lamb
comprising 8 cutlets
(backbone, skin and
most of fat removed,
ends of bones scraped)

2 sprigs parsley, 1 bay leaf,
1 sprig thyme (bouquet
garni)
2 large cloves garlic,
peeled, cut into slivers
1 cup lamb stock
2 tbsp butter
4 ripe tomatoes, peeled

---

Soak beans 6-8 hours or overnight, then drain, cover with water, add onions, seasoning and bouquet garni. Bring to boil then simmer gently until beans just tender. Drain, reserving liquid, and discard herbs. Chop onions finely, add to melted butter with tomatoes and juices, cook gently to a purée then add the beans and reheat, being careful not to break beans. Meanwhile, insert garlic slivers between eye of meat and bone, season and tie rack neatly. Cover with buttered tin foil and roast in preheated oven at 375°F. Bring stock to boil and use to baste lamb after 20 minutes cooking. Continue basting every 10 minutes for another half hour, discarding wrapping for last 10 minutes to brown lamb. When ready, keep warm. Add stock or bean water to sediment in pan, then add some of this gravy to bean mixture and place on a serving plate. Carve meat into cutlets, and serve on top of the beans with remaining meat stock handed round separately.

# Ratatouille

Compounded of all the flavours of Provence, this stew of peppers, eggplant, tomatoes and zucchini is redolent with the fragrant, lazy air of southern France.

---

*½ cup virgin olive oil*
*1 lb onions, finely sliced*
*1 lb tomatoes, skinned, deseeded and chopped, or can peeled, plum tomatoes with juices*
*1 lb eggplant, cut into 1 inch cubes*
*1 lb red and green peppers, stalks, seeds and pith discarded, cut into 1 inch pieces*
*2 cloves garlic, peeled and crushed with little salt*
*8 coriander seeds, crushed*
*3 parsley sprigs, a bay leaf, sprig of thyme, marjoram, tied together*
*salt & freshly ground black pepper*
*1 lb zucchini, cut into 1 inch thick slices*
*chopped basil or parsley*
*for serving cold: additional olive oil*

---

Heat oil gently, add onions and cook until well softened. Add tomatoes, cook until yielding juices then add the eggplant, peppers and flavourings and cook gently on top of stove, or in preheated oven at 350°F for 45 minutes. Add zucchini and cook 45 minutes more. Drain off juices and boil to reduce to syrupy liquid. Pour over vegetables, add the chopped basil or parsley and serve hot or cold.

# Gratin Dauphinois

A dish from the Dauphine region, this is a rich and wonderful way of eating potatoes. Larger quantities of potatoes need proportionately less cream. Try to use firm, waxy potatoes and cook in a shallow, earthenware container. Some versions add an egg and 1/4 cup grated Gruyère cheese, making it even richer.

| | |
|---|---|
| 1 1/2 lbs waxy potatoes, peeled and cut into 1/8 inch thick rounds | 4 tbsp butter |
| | salt & freshly ground black pepper |
| clove garlic, peeled | 1 cup heavy cream |

Rinse potato slices thoroughly to remove excess starch, pat dry in a clean cloth then layer in a shallow gratin dish which has been rubbed with a clove of garlic and well buttered. Season lightly as you go then pour over the cream, dot the remaining butter over the top, cover with tin foil and cook in a preheated oven at 300°F for about 1 1/2 hours, until really tender. Remove foil and turn oven up to 375°F for last 10 minutes to produce a golden crust. Serve with the simplest of meats and a green salad, or on its own before the meat, in which case you may like to increase the above quantities for 4 hungry people. For 3 lbs potatoes, use just over 1 1/2 cups cream.

# Tarte Tatin

This famous dessert was devised by two sisters, the demoiselles Tatin, at their inn in the hunting area of Solagne, a district of moors and lakes, at the end of the last century.

---

| | |
|---|---|
| 1 ¼ cups flour | 2 lbs crisp apples, |
| 1 ½ tbsp superfine sugar | peeled, cored and |
| pinch salt | quartered or cut in |
| ½ cup butter, chilled and | thick slices |
| diced | ¼ cup butter |
| 2 tbsp ice-cold water | ¼ cup superfine sugar |

---

Mix flour, sugar and salt, rub in butter until mixture resembles breadcrumbs then mix to a firm dough with the water. Leave to rest. Take an 8 inch baking dish and smear with half the second lot of butter, particularly the base. Scatter half the remaining sugar over the bottom. Pile in apples, scatter with last of the sugar and dot with remaining butter. Roll out pastry and cover tart. Make a steam hole. Place dish in a preheated oven at 400°F for 35 minutes (use tin foil to cover pastry if it starts to darken too much). Then gently lift pastry and tilt dish to check that the juices are a syrupy brown (a glass dish will reveal all through the bottom). Cook a little longer if necessary, then loosen pastry and turn tart out, upside down, onto a serving dish. If the apples aren't nicely caramelized, sift over some confectioners' sugar and place under a hot grill for a few minutes. Serve hot, warm or cold with whipped cream.

# Petit Pots de Crème au Chocolat

| | |
|---|---|
| 2 cups milk | 2 tbsp strong black coffee |
| 1 vanilla bean | (optional) |
| 6 oz plain dark | 5 large egg yolks |
| chocolate | 3 tbsp superfine sugar |
| 4 tbsp water | |

(serves 6)

Add vanilla bean to milk, bring to boil and leave to infuse. Add chocolate to water and melt gently either over boiling water or direct heat. Beat egg yolks until thick and pale then beat in sugar. Add hot milk gradually to melted chocolate then pour mixture into beaten egg and sugar, stirring constantly. Blend well, strain, then three-quarters fill lightly-greased, small heat-proof chocolate pots or deep ramekins. Place in baking pan, add boiling water round containers and place pan in preheated oven at 350°F for approximately 30-40 minutes (time will depend on size of pot used and depth of mixture). Creams are ready when just set. Cool on a rack then chill. Whipped cream can be used to decorate if liked.

# Oeufs à la Neige

One of my favourite desserts. Despite the fact that it uses Crème Anglaise, it is found in most traditional French restaurants, though the meringue is often cooked in one piece. The combination of egg custard, poached meringue 'eggs' and the lacy caramel is perfection.

## Custard

| | |
|---|---|
| 2 cups milk | 4 large egg yolks |
| 1 vanilla bean or few drops vanilla extract | 1/2 cup sugar |

## Meringue 'Eggs'

| | |
|---|---|
| 3 large egg whites | 1/4 cup vanilla sugar |
| 2 tbsp granulated sugar | (or superfine sugar |
| few drops vanilla extract | plus few drops vanilla extract) |

## Caramel

| | |
|---|---|
| 10-12 sugar lumps | 1 tbsp water |

Heat milk with split vanilla bean to just below boiling point. Remove from heat, cover and leave to infuse 20 minutes, or add vanilla extract to hot milk. Beat egg yolks until thick and pale then beat in sugar by the tablespoon. Gradually beat in hot milk. Return to cleaned-out saucepan and gently cook, stirring constantly until mixture coats back of spoon. Allow to cool, stirring to prevent skin forming. Whip egg whites to stiff peak then whisk in vanilla sugar. Add the granulated sugar and a few drops vanilla extract to a sauté pan or shallow saucepan holding some 2 inch depth water. Bring to poaching point (surface of water should just shiver). Scoop out tablespoonfuls of meringue mixture and place on water. Allow to poach for 2 minutes then turn with a slotted spoon. Poach on other side for I minute. then remove to double-layer paper towels to drain. Poach as many eggs together as pan will comfortably hold, remembering they swell as they cook.

Place cooled custard in shallow dish and arrange 'eggs' on top. Put sugar lumps in small saucepan, sprinkle with water; heat steadily until sugar is melted and caramelized to golden brown. Immediately trickle this over eggs in lacy pattern. Chill dish until ready to serve.

# Vin Chaud aux Épices

It is not necessary to use a vintage wine for this recipe. A young Beaujolais is ideal. A drink for wintry evenings.

| | |
|---|---|
| 4 cups red wine | 8 almonds, unblanched |
| ½ cup sugar | I cinnamon stick |
| I eating apple, sliced | 4 cloves |
| I orange, quartered | 6 tbsp rum or brandy |

Heat wine with all ingredients except the spirits, bring to boil and allow to reduce for 10 minutes. Remove from heat, cover pan and allow to infuse for 5 minutes. Strain, add rum or brandy, reheat gently if necessary, then serve.